Unicorns and Donuts: The Art of Cannabis Sales
A Guide for Businesses, Sales Managers, and Sales Reps in the Cannabis Industry
By: Nina Faull, MBA

Unicorns and Donuts: The Art of Cannabis Sales
A Guide for Businesses, Sales Managers, and Sales Reps in the Cannabis Industry
©2018 Nina Faull
All Rights Reserved

Table of Contents

- Preface
- A Brief Introduction
- The Skinny on the Business of Cannabis
- Who is Your Ideal Target Market
- Cannabis Sales
  - Hierarchy of Sales From the Client's Perspective
  - The Beginnings of a Sales Pitch
  - Sales Team Resources
  - The Pop-Up
  - The Roll of Emails and Phone Calls in Cannabis Sales
- Sales Management
  - Sales Goal Metric
- Customer Relationship Management System (CRM)
- Hiring Sales Reps
  - Unicorn of Sales Reps
- Being a Cannabis Sales Rep
  - Used Car Salesmen
  - Actually Being a Cannabis Sales Rep
  - A Sales Rep's Book of Business
  - Numbers, Numbers, Numbers
- In Closing
- A Couple of Resources

Preface

What makes cannabis great is that you can apply the corporate principles that work, and leave out all the details that make "corporate" a bad word. This is the industry to cultivate a positive, fun culture. That's what cannabis is all about.

This book may seem simple and should be "common sense," but because I've seen, first-hand, cannabis companies ignore these sales basics, not willfully, but because cannabis has presented us with many young and talented business owners who may not have the most robust sales background. So, I felt it was time to provide valuable input from inside the industry.

At the very least, I implore business owners and senior management to pay close attention to the metrics I use in the Sales Management section of this handbook, as they will help put your entire business in perspective and assist you making accurate projections and properly structure the expectations of your sales team.

A Brief Introduction

So, who am I and why should you trust me?

Well, I was a highly successful medical sales rep for a decade, and realized that my passion just wasn't in medicine. Honestly, I hated it. In many ways the industry was soulless, patients are numbers and the greed is rampant. Doctors are political, and the better connected they are, the more they influence lobbyists. Then there's the plight of the sales reps. Reps are the first to get commissions cut when new regulations come to pass, no matter how hard they work, if the company is losing money, commissions get cut to maintain the income of senior management, I could go on and on.

I've owned my own food industry business and applied my medical sales techniques, and they worked. After five years of grinding 7 days a week, attending national trade shows, working with brokers, PR agencies, and gaining placement in national stores, restaurants, and university kitchens, I thought I was well on my way. But as we all know, it takes many years and a lot of money to establish a brand and gain customers. When my company needed further investment, I had to make a tough decision - spend more money or apply my talents to something I'm passionate about. So I did the latter. But what was I passionate about? I was passionate about cannabis. It helped me with anxiety from the first day I tried it and I found that my use of it was not only enjoyable, but therapeutic. So, I tipped my toe in and consulted in the cannabis industry. I quickly saw that many companies didn't have the many of the necessary resources to properly support their sales team, nor the sales experience to properly guide them. I was a desirable candidate because they knew my experience would yield results. They wanted to pay "commission only" which is hardly livable, even if I was just starting out in my career, the structure wouldn't allow me to survive. They had little to no brand awareness, and very little "swag," to help the sales department spark conversations. So, I kept looking.

My first real foray into cannabis sales was for a poorly structured company, with a seemingly endless bankroll and a Chief Operations Officer with no business background. The company offered a paltry salary, poorly structured commissions, and unrealistic sales goals. I accepted the position for the experience and rather than complaining, I set out to help the company understand the true nature of sales.

In 90 days, I increased the performance of a remarkably small territory by 300%, but they still wanted more. Their sales goals were extremely unrealistic, as they were weighing each territory equally and only based their goals on company need, rather than realistic territory yield. As I set out to assist the company in developing more realistic expectations, I asked for the metric on how they came up with their goals, when they couldn't supply that, I asked for the marketing part of their business plan. Their response was, "we haven't gotten there yet." I was baffled as to how they achieved investment dollars with so little information, but instead of arguing, I decided to supply them with the reality, with the hope of making an impression and guiding them to a more structured approach. So I did my own market research and presented them with the results. (I'll go more into the strategy and metric I used in this handbook.)

Needless to say, my efforts did very little in the immediate moment. I had given my notice, as I had been offered a new job with a company whom I thought could better use my expertise. About 2 weeks after I left, I received a call from my former supervisor, as well as two fellow sales reps. Apparently, the new Sales Director went into my old territory to "see for himself." The reality was, he went into the territory to prove me wrong, but in the end he acknowledged, in their sales meeting that, "Nina was right."

Yes, I felt a bit vindicated, but at the same time, my greatest hope was that this was a wake up call to cannabis companies to run their business like a business.

I've been contemplating whether or not I should share with you my recent cannabis experience. I've found that it isn't an unfamiliar story to many in the industry, so I've decided to supply a brief overview.

As I mentioned, I left my cannabis product sales job for a job with an "ancillary" business. They were an advertising company for brands and dispensaries. It was a good platform, perhaps a bit too new for the industry, but I believed in it. I knew, going into this company, that my biggest challenges would be explaining the value of what we were offering to businesses, as well as changing buyer behavior to gain cannabis customers. I had my strategy and set to work immediately.

In the beginning, the financials with which I was presented were solid and indicated that the company had money to support operations while we grew. It seemed to make sense that the bulk of the company's money was spent on tech but I would find out less than a year later, they left little, if anything, for sales and marketing. For 9 months I worked nearly 7 days a week, heading the charge of the national sales efforts. I closed deals in other states for my reps, while simultaneously closing deals in Colorado. I was given little more than some company information, stickers, and pins, and despite my reps' efforts, I was the only one to ever bring in paying subscriptions. How did I do it? My reputation. In my previous job, I had built solid relationships with a variety of personalities in the industry. They knew they could trust me, because I make it a point not to let people down and stand behind my word. People entrusted me with their money, as I promised *and delivered* the help they needed. The tech we had didn't have many users, but I hustled every day to show the value to my clients and their customers.

Fast forward a few months and things started getting weird. Amidst major company upheaval, I learned an excessive amount of bad business practices were being used and even more were being implemented. Even though I was bringing in results and was complemented many times on my efforts and performance, I knew something was amiss, and even found myself faced with a moral and ethical crisis. How could I continue to sell a product for leadership who was proving false? I couldn't come up with an answer, so I knew I had to find a new job and make my exit quickly. In the meantime, I kept my head down and my mouth shut. Inevitably, the company opted to "terminate my contract" before I was able to secure a new job, which was fine with me, as my integrity was more valuable than my position.

Throughout my experience in business, I've seen a lot of underhanded tactics, some worse than others, and I quickly learned that many in the cannabis industry have been exposed to varying levels of corporate greed, and shady business. I'm not saying that all investors in the cannabis space have a greedy mentality, there are many who are looking to make sound investments in the industry. However, there are also many investors and "business" people who have sorted pasts and are seeking a "quick flip" investment opportunity. The problem for these types of people is, this industry seems to vet out corporate sleeze. Once discovered, and it always gets discovered, the tightly bound cannabis community cuts them off at the knees. The reality is, too many people have risked too much to be bilked. Cannabis is personal. It's taken a long time to see days like this, many people in this industry have been imprisoned, fined, ridiculed and so much more. All of this makes cannabis a tight-knit industry of people on a mission, and trust is paramount.

***

Unicorns and Donuts: The Art of Cannabis Sales
A Guide for Businesses, Sales Managers, and Sales Reps in the Cannabis Industry

The Skinny on the Business of Cannabis

Cannabis is an industry full of people who want to help others. Whether their attitude is "it's safer than alcohol," or seniors using it to reduce pain medication, both recreational and medical dispensaries see every type of individual imaginable and they want to help. So if you're thinking about entering the cannabis space, make sure your offering helps them achieve their goals. I don't know how to say this in any other way, this industry is like nothing you've ever seen. It's unique and it's finding its way, if you're trying to apply your heavy-handed business savvy, you will likely get pushed out, as industry professionals and cannabis customers do not function like you. They are driven by passion for this very unique and diverse plant, not the perception that cannabis is going to make them rich.

Cannabis is the industry of weed, NOT an industry of greed.

Trust is what cannabis is all about. Customers trust dispensaries and brands to help them, and dispensaries and brands trust their partners to help them grow awareness so they can deliver wellness to their customers. It's a very positive life cycle that businesses should acknowledge. You hear very little about "making money" when talking with dispensary owners and staff. Yes, they want customers and need to cover their expenses, but you will always hear them talk about "taking care of their patients/customers" as well as "taking care of their staff."

I hear a lot of people say that the biggest challenge for cannabis is that it's Federally illegal and faced with so many regulations. I don't disagree, but I believe those items to be symptoms of a bigger issue. In my humble opinion, after working closely in the cannabis industry for a few years, the reality is, the cannabis industry is still figuring out where it fits into the bigger picture.

The primary issue the industry faces is actually, "How does the Cannabis Community tear down the walls of the stigma that has endured for nearly a century and find its place in the mainstream?"

Finding the answer to this question will create demand, but until then, cannabis advocacy groups and individuals are left with the tough job of guerrilla marketing and public relations. While public perception will naturally influence demand for cannabis businesses, the cannabis business community is simultaneously trying to figure out where cannabis fits into the bigger picture of business, and many cannabis businesses are also trying to figure out how they should operate, all while navigating the rules and regulations imposed by the politicians they elected.

The one thing the Cannabis Community doesn't have to worry about is culture. The people of the industry embrace people from all walks of life. They laugh and they play. They are passionate and some of the best people I've ever encountered in my career.

Cannabis business owners span many generations, young and old, and each of them truly believes in their mission to help people, whether that help is simply to have fun or reduce a dependence on opiates. Whatever the passion, it is a driving force. However, that doesn't necessarily imply business savvy, and there are thousands of "consultants" who would love the opportunity to make money in cannabis. The only thing is, cannabis doesn't necessarily operate like any other industry. Sure, the basic business principles are the same, but again, cannabis is a culture. The need for professionals with the ability and desire to become part of a very unique and diverse community is essential, and from what I've seen, this combination is bit rare.

Novice is both an asset and detriment to the cannabis industry. There are many in cannabis management trying to "prove themselves" so they run over their team with arrogance, which is simply a symptom of being in a position of power for the first time in their life.

My first piece of advice is simple, don't do this.

If you want to nurture a positive culture that yields results, work with your team as an asset, not as disposable cogs in a wheel.

***
Who is Your Ideal Target Market?

Before you even think about launching your business, applying for licensure, securing a facility, and everything else that goes into the actual production of your products, you must complete your business plan. This is Business 101, so if you're exploring launching a company, you already know this. You should also know that your business plan is where you define your product's category (flower, edibles, concentrates, topicals, etc.). You will need to know your category to perform industry research and make projections, so be sure you know where your products fit in the market. Your business plan is also where you begin to vet your ideas and costs, which will lead to a clear picture of your product's viability in any industry. Marketing will, of course, have its place in your business plan, and sales falls under the same umbrella. They're different, but there's a synergy between the two.

Since this book is a handbook for cannabis sales, I won't go any further on your business plan. There are many resources in the market for helping build a solid plan. But before I go much further, I want to touch on something I've seen happen, and it doesn't make much sense. Not to mention, it's a detriment to your sales efforts, and overall company performance, which is why I feel the need to mention it. Know your cost of goods, production costs, salaries, including your own, other overhead costs (including delivery fees), profit margin, and the percentage of commission to your reps *BEFORE* you go into business or launch an additional product. Just because your product is great, doesn't mean it won't price itself out of the market. Oh, and also include a hefty budget for "penny samples" for your prospective clients. They're going to want to try your products before they buy them.

Something else I've seen companies do that is detrimental to sales performance, which inevitably reflects in company performance is - launching a new product, having it sell incredibly well, only to find out months later that they're actually losing money on it. In quick reaction, they did a massive price increase, to cover the actual costs, and lost business immediately. This looks bad on not only the company, but on your reps, as well. If you're product is too expensive to produce, but you absolutely insist on producing it because it's the next "best thing," and you feel that with traction you can capitalize on economies of scale discounts in the near future, start small, super small. Expect to take a loss, but also use it as a chance to perform your own market research (i.e.: who is buying your product? Why do they like it? How can you make it better?).

Many perceive that "anything cannabis" is in high demand and companies simply identify their target market as "every cannabis user." Well, that's just not good enough. You must hone this in, as the finer details will be necessary as you develop a cohesive sales pitch that will be successful. Revisiting your business and marketing plan every quarter is a good idea in the beginning; once you have traction in the market, revisiting it once or twice a year is also a good idea. You'll find that as you get closer to launching your product, and after your product is in the hands of consumers, your target market will begin to evolve. Revisiting your business plan will allow your company to evolve, as well.

So, now that you know your costs, let's start attacking your target market. Ask yourself the following question:

"Is this product meant to be an "everyday" product or a "boutique" product?

The reason I mention this first is because everyday products must be inexpensive at the Point of Sale (POS). Boutique products are desirable, but will likely take longer to gain traction, as higher prices are not always desirable when customers can buy a product that will do exactly what they need for $2 - $5 less, and the customer already knows they love it. Believe me, $2 makes a difference in this industry. So, while you're doing research make sure you look into how your dispensaries apply mark up. A general rule of thumb is to assume dispensaries will simply double the wholesale price. That said, if you plan to sell your product for $15 wholesale, is the end user willing to pay $30? If so, who are the people willing to pay it?

As the example states, based on your knowledge of your production and distribution costs, you must consider your potential retail price, and define who is willing to pay it. This will help you better define your target market. And these answers are *not* about your opinion, which is subjective, it's about doing your research and providing factual support for your answers. If you're going to be successful in cannabis, or any business, you must start with taking a hard, honest look at these basic, yet informative, types of questions. As your answers are going to support the sales pitch and sales goals you will implement.

In the beginning, your product is obviously new and relatively unknown, and as the example shows, if a customer can pay $2 less for a product they know they like, then your products won't immediately sell. (We'll talk about overcoming this in the Sales

Strategy section of this handbook.) If you're shooting for a "boutique" market, then you can charge more, but your packaging, product's overall presentation, taste, and efficacy should represent something worth the extra money. You should also expect it to take longer to gain traction in the market.

You should note that very few brands actually know what's being charged for their products at the Point of Sale, and often don't know if the savings of reduced wholesale prices are passed onto the customer, so do your "secret shopper" research. As I mentioned, most dispensaries simply double the wholesale cost, but that's not a guarantee, maybe they'll charge more, maybe they'll charge less. Using the "double the wholesale" rule-of-thumb is good but as I'll continue to say, research. Involve your sales reps in your research. They're the front lines of your business and their network will likely yield a lot of valuable information, i.e.: new products entering your category space, do your competitors have minimum wholesale orders, do they charge delivery fees (NOTE: most do not charge delivery, unless minimum orders haven't been met). You must be vigilant about knowing who your direct competitors are, what customers are paying for their products, are your competitors' products on sale (this may indicate a bulk purchase discount), what are the demographics of those customers - age, gender, income levels, etc. If you're lucky, your reps' networks may even yield wholesale pricing on your competition, but this is a bold request. So tread lightly with this, often times assuming the "double the wholesale price" is best.

Overall, this research will help you define your product's image - "everyday" or "boutique" and help you begin to make an educated decision on your target market. Here's an example of a target market that will assist your sales department begin to formulate a pitch that will help train their reps and be the foundation for their individual sales approach.

30-40 year old females, business professionals with disposable income, highly engaged cannabis consumers, interested in cannabis for whole-body wellness

Since you now know who you're talking to, you can begin to develop your sales strategy and pitch.

***

Cannabis Sales

Hierarchy of Sales From the Client's Perspective

1. Sales Representative

The Sales Representative is an advocate for both the company and the client. It's a fine line reps must walk to ensure that their clients are receiving the product, information, and satisfaction they need to continuing doing business with the company. The rep is the first person the client calls when they need to order, they're also the first person they call when something goes wrong…whether it's between the client and the company, or the client has a dissatisfied customer. You're sales reps are your front line for conflict resolution. Oh, and sales reps are almost never called when something goes right.

2. Your Products

Your products are not only a direct reflection on your company, but they're a direct reflection on your sales reps. If your products are consistent and never falter, then you're rep's job should be easy. But it your products' THC testing is on the low-end of the allowable variance, you're essentially shorting customers their high and patients their medication. It's not acceptable, and your rep will pay the price with rejected orders, fewer reorders, and word will spread that your products aren't "that great." Companies often try to make these instances right, but it's up to your rep to perform damage control, which is wasted time and money. Best to just get things right the first time.

3. Your Company

To the client, the company is, well, faceless. Often times, they still reach out to their old reps, even after they've changed companies; that's how deep a rep's ties can go. Yet, most companies always think that a rep is a reflection on them, which is true, but the other reality is, when you're an outside sales rep, your company is also a reflection on you. It's all about your rep being able to back up their word with support from your company. In the best case, clients won't hold the rep accountable for a bad experience, but rest-assured, the rep will feel the wrath if the company messes up. Fewer orders are always the consequence of a bad company interaction. So if a client feels wronged, and you don't help the rep find a middle-of-the-road solution, can you truly blame the rep for a reduction in orders? Nope. You can't.

***

The Beginnings of a Sales Pitch

I'm not the biggest fan of having scripts for sales reps. Each rep has their own unique voice and brings their own unique skillset to the company. You hired them because you felt they had the skillset necessary to sell your products, so let them do what you hired them to do. Every sales rep must be given the autonomy to use their own words when pitching your company.

Note I said "company" and not "products." This is because sales reps must have a solid understanding of the company's mission, because this is the first item to communicate, before they even begin to pitch your product. People are going to want to know exactly what you do, what you stand for, and where you're from. I'm also not talking about the company's "Mission Statement." I'm talking about two or three sentences which define your company. For example,

The Cannabis Gourmet team is driven by passion for consistently infusing oils which can be used in every adult's diet to work cannabis into their overall wellness routine. Our founders are experienced cannabis chefs, and our recipes have been vigorously tested to ensure flavor, depth, and potency.

Sales reps rarely have more than a minute or two to communicate why they're standing in front of their clients. This is why this statement must be clear, concise, and succinctly convey the message. If these few statements can do all of this for your sales team, your reps should have no problem drawing from it when they're communicating with prospective clients. This is why there's no need to go into the extensive bios of the founders, and other details that aren't pertinent to their initial company training. It acts more as a guideline, rather than a script. The reality is, this statement provides your reps need just enough information to begin their understanding of exactly what you do and why you do it. The questions they encounter in the field will help them dive deeper, and they will retain more of the "hands on" information than they would sitting and reading lengthy training information.

Once a rep knows the message the company wishes to disseminate to the masses, they will need to know the key attributes of your products. This includes:

- Type of product - "everyday" or "boutique"

- What makes products different from competitor's?
- Production Processes
  - Where ingredients/flower is sourced
  - Best practices used to ensure quality and consistency
  - Are products strain specific?
  - How are products infused?
- Extraction processes (if applicable)
- Ingredients (if applicable)
  - Unique attributes of ingredients
- Testing
  - Potency results for each batch
  - Terpene profiles
- Packaging sizes
- Company Images and Logos, and the inspiration for each
- Where packaging is sourced (from cannabis friendly states, vendors, etc.)
  - Is packaging recyclable
- Order Fulfillment Timeline
- Wholesale Pricing Sheets
- Discounts Available

Information is key in sales and tools should be available as a reference, not necessarily a "leave behind" for customers, as these get lost, thrown away, or simply buried under the other countless pieces of sales material dispensaries receive. Memorization in sales comes with time, as there's a lot of information to learn. There's no sense in a sales rep spending time reading, when their money is made in the field working. Therefore, once your reps have a firm grasp (note I didn't say "solid grasp") of your company's mission and product offering, reps should be encouraged to get out in the field and start doing their jobs. It's expected that they'll stumble a bit, that's the nature of repping a new product. No amount of time in an office studying is going to solve for this. Encourage them to say "I'm not sure, but I'll find out," if they encounter a question they can't answer. These are valuable learning opportunities and the information they glean from your replies will stay with them for the length of their employment. Plus, cannabis businesses are always happy to have a follow up if a question can't be answered immediately. These are amazing opportunities that are the foundation for building strong relationships. Sales reps will encounter a multitude of questions in the field, if you're hearing the same question from various reps, you'll know that you need to add a resource to your sales reps' arsenal.

Another important note is that cannabis sales is not a formal sales pitch that you might see in other industries, it's always a conversation - a flow between your rep and their prospect. Which is another reason why I hate scripted pitches. But, if you absolutely insist on giving them a script, let it begin and end with, "Hi, my name is So and So. I'm from Cannabis Gourmet. I wasn't sure who to speak with about getting you some samples of our line of infused cooking oils."

Speaking of samples. Sampling your products to your reps is always a good idea, as they will bring their own experiences into conversations about your products to their clients. Every interaction with your product will assist in your sales team's understanding and get them excited about your product, which is the first step to gaining placement on dispensary shelves.

Remember, as you learn new information as to the benefits of your products - i.e.: potency testing, a new way of extraction, etc., be sure to inform your reps. Sales reps, above all, need to know everything about your product to make a solid pitch that will allow your product to stand on its own when customers try it. Word spreads quickly in this industry. If you have a great product, it will begin to sell itself. If you have an average product, remove your ego and pride, you should view this is a good thing. Acknowledging that your product doesn't stand up to your competition's is an opportunity for you to make improvements.

Sales Team Resources

Let's say that everything is perfect - you've got a solid understanding of your business and ideal customers, where it fits in the cannabis market, a fantastic product that has been rigorously vetted against the competition, great margins, an awesome brand image, and money saved to be invested in sales and marketing. Here's a list of things your sales team will need, and believe me, I've seen sales forces in cannabis go out without even a business card - bad idea.

- Business Cards
- Brochures (these can be digital for email attachments, extra paper isn't always desirable in cannabis)
- Die-cut Stickers (these are huge in cannabis and should be in constant supply)
- Branded Swag
  - Lanyards
  - Industry Badge Holders (to hang from lanyards)
  - Custom Hat Pins (great to display on industry professionals' lanyards)
  - T-Shirts
  - Embroidered Hats
  - Water Bottles

- Sunglasses
- Pens
- Sticky Notes
- Dab Mats
- Banner Stands (for events)
- Branded Table Cover
- Engaging Table Signs that draw customer attention and spark a conversation
- Sample Packaging Displays
- Foldable 4' Tables

(Resources for purchasing these products are at the back of this handbook.)

The Pop Up (AKA: Vendor Day)

You'll often find cannabis product sales reps staging "Pop Ups," or more formally referred to as "Vendor Days." These are small table set ups at dispensaries during peak hours, promoting their company's products to customers as they walk through the door. Pop Ups are necessary to begin informing customers and dispensaries about the value of your new, amazing product. They're the way to begin showing value for your product, and explain why your product is worth the cost. They are also chock full of swag (see items listed above) and stickers. And believe me, customers love free stuff! These are great for brand awareness, even if they don't buy your product that day. If you make a favorable impression on the customer, they will be more inclined to purchase another time. The goal is brand awareness and future business, not always an immediate sale. (See Used Car Salesmen Need Not Apply Section.)

Most of the time, during a Pop-Up, there's a "limited time deal" going on while the company's representative is there. This is both appealing to the customer as well as the dispensary, but keep in mind, any discounts aren't going to come from the dispensary during Pop-Ups, you'll have to either supply them with extra product or credit their next invoice, whichever follows your state's rules and regulations for discounted cannabis products.

There are various cannabis brand ambassador companies in legal states who are able to help with Pop-Ups, and because Pop-Ups are so desirable to your dispensaries, this avenue is often more cost-effective than pulling your reps from the field to perform these. Generally, though, most sales reps do perform their own Pop-Ups. In my opinion, it's best to have a company rep at these events. First, they can make sure that the product is being sold correctly, it gives them a chance to observe buyer behavior, do a bit of their own market research, but moreover, it puts them in front of the dispensary's management team, which are usually who they need to follow-up with, address concerns, get reorders, etc.

In some ways, Pop-Ups are more like marketing than sales, but the line between these two departments is often blurred. That said, it's extremely wise that you keep your sales team informed as to your company's marketing efforts, such as sponsorships, as your reps can use this information to have a new, fresh reason to see a client again, and create some excitement around the event.

The Roll of Emails and Phone Calls in Cannabis Sales

After all my years in sales, I have yet to start a viable conversation and gain commitments from "cold call" emails. Same goes for phone sales. The reality is, prospective customers are just like you and me. They get inundated with emails every day from people asking for their business. It's just as easy to hit delete than read a lengthy email about your wonderful company and your products, as it is to say, "I'm not interested right now," and hang up. If someone really wants their business, they will have to do it the old fashioned way, by getting out of the house/office, driving to their location, and starting a conversation. If a rep wants to make a preliminary phone call to find out the best time to stop by, that's respectable, as many dispensary employees and owners work random hours. But dispensary employees and owners also work long days, and a lengthy phone conversation is never desirable.

That said, there is a place for emails and phone calls in cannabis sales, and that place is follow up. The stronger the relationship your rep has built, the more efficient they can be in using these tools to secure new and repeat orders.

And this leads me to handouts. In some industries, printed literature, otherwise known as "leave behinds" are extremely effective, but from my experience in cannabis, literature does very little until *after* a client has begun ordering your products. Even then, an informational handout should have extremely valid information that can be used to assist the dispensary's customer, not necessarily the dispensary, themselves. Handouts are just more clutter in a world of state paperwork, invoices, product tags, etc. If your reps are going to leave anything behind, let it be stickers. The cannabis industry *loves* stickers.

This doesn't mean that you shouldn't have some kind of literature available to your reps, though. It never hurts to have relevant attachments that reps can use to enhance their emails. Remember, it's all about reps having *resources*, but those resources won't always be necessary, but they do come in handy at the appropriate time.

***

Sales Management

Now, Before We Talk About Your Reps, Let's Talk About Sales Management

Sales managers have a million things to do - run reports, establish goals, performance reviews, etc. First thing's first - understand that it takes an average of 6 months for a sales rep to develop a territory. More seasoned reps may achieve this quicker. Next, when developing sales goals, make them challenging, but don't just plug in random numbers based on what you and/or the company needs to see. Make educated decisions on your sales goals by using the following metric.

Sales Goal Metric

Below is the metric that I used to help my previous company develop more realistic sales goals for my territory. (This is probably where I should note that I hate word problems, but they do come in handy at times like this.)

For simplicities sake, let's start with one dispensary where we sold our edible products. I wanted to know how much they could realistically purchase from me.

Dispensary X has $100,000 in gross sales per month
Edible sales account for 50% of their monthly sales and they carry 10 different edible products
Based on this, they make $50,000 per month on edibles
They carry 10 different brands, but 4 brands make up 50% of that $50,000 ($25,000) and the remaining 6 brands make up the other $25,000
Since I knew that the best selling brands sold a total of $25,000 per month, or $6,250 per brand, the other 6 edible products each sold $4,167 per month.

Using the "double the wholesale price" rule-of-thumb, I could presume that the best selling edibles each received $3,125 per month in orders and the less popular edibles received $2,084 in orders. So, the most I could make from Dispensary X, if my product was among the most popular, would be $3,125 per month.

***

Now, we're going to look at a territory of 100 dispensaries, which means we have to factor in a realistic percentage of dispensaries that will carry your product. By the way, it's never 100%, ever.

Let's say you wanted to challenge your reps to have 60% market share, because your product is better than donuts. So, of these 100 dispensaries, you are challenging your rep to achieve placement in 60 of them. But how much money will you make?

100 dispensaries make about $1,000,000 in gross sales per month
Edible sales account for an average of 75% of monthly sales
These 100 dispensaries carry an average of 20 different edible products, 5 of these brands make up 50% of their sales, while the other 15 make up the other 50%

Based on this, the territory of 100 dispensaries makes $750,000 per month on edibles
[$1M x 75%]
There are 20 different brands carried in this territory, but 5 brands earn 50% of sales, so the "Top 5" are responsible for $375,000 in sales, or $75,000 per brand
The other 15 less popular edible brands are responsible for the remaining $375,000, or $25,000 per brand
Using the "double the wholesale price" rule-of-thumb, you can presume that the "Top 5" receive about $37,500 in wholesale orders each month, and the less popular brands each receive about $12,500 in monthly orders
This is the total wholesale territory yield for edibles, if you had 100% of the dispensaries purchasing your products…

But you don't…

You're only banking on 60% placement, so the math specific to your business is as follows:

60% of 100 dispensaries is 60 dispensaries
60% of $1,000,000 in gross sales per month is $600,000
75% of edible sales for your 60 dispensaries is $450,000 per month
20 different brands sold in those 60 dispensaries, 5 brands are responsible for 50% of edible sales, so the Top 5 in your 60 dispensaries sell about $225,000, or $45,000 per brand, and the other 15 brands make up the other $225,000 per month, or $15,000 per brand
Which means,
If you are among the Top 5, you can project that the *wholesale* for this territory would yield $22,500 per month, if you're among the other 15 brands, you could project $7,500 per month.

Even if you were in the Top 5, you now have a realistic idea of how this example territory will influence your company's bottom line. The investment for your compliant facility as well as licensure, for an edible company, is upwards of $100,000 or more, depending on your state, facility costs, etc., and that's before a single product is produced. $22,500 per month for a generous market share really isn't that much. Keep this in mind as you embark on your cannabis business and sales journey.

***

Just because the company is running low on money, or has to report big numbers to investors, all parties must understand that growth takes time. The perception that cannabis is "flying off the shelves" is a misnomer. It's highly competitive, heavily regulated, and as in any industry, it takes time to develop a reputation. Make sure company budgets are prepared to endure slow sales in the beginning. Reps must be able to achieve their goals, or at least get close to reaching them, if they are to stay motivated.

Speaking of motivation...

The key to running a successful sales team is to make being part of that team a requirement for managers. If a sales manager is always dictating and harping on numbers, it's very much the opposite of motivating. Reps will work hard for you if they are treated respectfully and know that this is a team effort. So, if management has all the answers, they should be willing to get out there and work side-by-side with their team. Not necessarily every day, but it is essential to lead a sales team from the front. Pick a small territory or some larger "corporate" accounts and show your reps that it *can* be done, and goals can be met. Let them learn from your quality techniques, and be open to learning from theirs. Moreover, this will also give managers insight as to the challenges their reps face, which should be used to strategize how to overcome them. What I'm saying is, sales management is more of an advocate for the sales force than it is a heavy hand willing to fire people at any given turn.

That said...

In an industry struggling to find itself, there's no need to rule with an iron fist. Please remember that sales is not an 8 - 5 job. Often times, it's a 15 hour day, reps check emails on weekends, vacations, they network even when they're out to drinks with their friends. Sales is a lifestyle, so please do not, I repeat, do not assume that sales is just a "fun time job" and that your reps aren't working. It can be grueling at times, not to mention the frustration of traffic jams and car troubles. Your reps shouldn't dread your phone calls because all you do is beat them up about numbers, daily. You'll know by a rep's interaction with you and the team, and their numbers, if they're working. Your job is to motivate reps and ensure that their job is engaging. Yes, numbers matter, but the *quality* of your sales strategy and tools matter just as much. Coach them, using the expertise that got you to your position, that's your job.

Above all, listen to your reps. Unless specifically asked, it's rare that a rep will speak up if the techniques they use are working. Reps are more likely to speak up when the pitch or product are met with opposition and all too often, I've heard management refer to these "cries for help" as "excuses" as to why a particular rep simply can't sell the product. These are *NOT* excuses. This is valuable feedback; these are opportunities for the sales department and management to be creative to overcome barriers. Reps who are not working or not working to the best of their ability will rarely have quality feedback, the ones who are talking, offering feedback and suggestions, are the ones who are working the hardest. Taking a global approach, assessing numbers and feedback, is the first step to solving the problem. It's a lot less expensive than simply firing a rep because you *think* they're not working. Educate yourself.

I know it seems that I'm advising on what not to do in Sales Management, and honestly, it doesn't stop there...

Limit the amount of time you "ride with your reps." You hired them because you trust that they are good at working both individually and as a team. Unless there's a specific concern or meeting, this is a great way to make things extremely awkward and interrupt the flow of their relationships. In most cases, this tactic reeks of micromanagement and insult. If you do go into your reps' accounts, make sure they're with you, you don't want to undercut your team. And don't try to show them how to "wheel and deal," it's seedy and attempts to show that you have the "upper hand." It's their territory and their reputation, you're only there to enhance them, not show off.

> *You want your efforts to complement your reps, not complicate them.*

If you're trying to figure out why a territory isn't yielding, or would like to make better, more realistic sales projections and goals, ask each of your reps to help perform the research, within their respective territories, for the metrics you use to determine their sales goals.

They will need to survey the dispensaries in their territory for the following information:

- Total number of accounts in their territory, noting how many of these are actively ordering from them
- Gross monthly sales in as many accounts as will provide this information
- Approximate percentage of monthly sales for your category, in each of their accounts
- How many brands in your category, in each account
- Percentage of business each brand represents within the category, in each account

Then it's all simple math. Have your reps create a spreadsheet which lists each account in their territory and columns to represent each of the parameters you requested. Add each column up and find its average. They can then send this to their manager for further analysis.

This exercise provides not only management, but the sales rep, with a solid understanding of their territory dynamics. It encourages your sales team to take ownership of their respective territories, and challenges the reps to take the necessary steps to further their career. Remember, you're building your reps into people you don't want to lose…you're building them into valuable company assets.

***

Customer Relationship Management (CRM) System

My sales career began before CRMs were a common tool in a sales team. I tracked my business and sales the old way, by hand, and then by spreadsheet. I found this to be the best way to truly dive into my strategies and my customer relationships. When CRMs became mainstream, I quickly learned that this is a great way to micromanage the team and see if they're doing their jobs. As you can probably guess, I've never been a big fan of this tactic. Reps are judged by their numbers, you'll know by orders if your reps are performing. CRM's are best used as tools for sales reps to log their notes and thoughts, so they can revisit them when it's time for follow up and brush up on where they left off. They're also a great way for management to reference what's going on in a given territory and use them to assist in improving sales strategies and performance.

Any sales rep worth their salt will not rely solely on a CRM to track their accounts. That said, I know my words aren't going to change the fact that the CRM will be looked at daily to see who's doing what. Sales reps are best to keep their own records on their orders and accounts, track orders on a spreadsheet, and cross reference the CRM. If you're smart, your reps have signed an Non-Disclosure Agreement, so this information isn't expected to go any further, but it safe guards the rep from potential tampering in a CRM. I've seen it happen, CRM accounts get mis-assigned, deleted, etc., whether it's a system error, honest mistake, or straight out tampering, it's essential that reps protect themselves and track their own performance. Your encouragement of this secondary technique shows that you and the company are honest and seek to protect your employees.

As reps develop themselves, they are developing their personal "book of business." It is expected that the contacts be reported to their employer, however, this is another way reps develop their own reputation. As we already know, sales is about relationships, which are, in reality, "friendships." I still have many many friends whom I met years ago throughout my medical career, they know me as a professional and as a person. These are important relationships which I value. Again, sales is not a "job," it is their life. If a rep has a good relationship, it will lead to your company's good reputation. It follows them, not your company.

Remember, businesses are doing business with your rep, not your company. Reps walk a line between the customer and company. They are an advocate for both.

Essentially, this is the law of natural consequence. Businesses should see this as a rep's asset, and as I mentioned, they should work to nurture and develop a rep that they don't want to lose. Cannabis is a small industry. If a rep has a track record of success and strong relationships, whether they built them during their employment with you or not, and things go sour, you *will* lose business, whether they tell their tale of disenchantment or not. New reps will have a hard time filling big shoes. Repairing collateral damage is time consuming, which is money lost. So allow your reps the time to build relationships, and provide them with the resources to make a great first impression and nurture a culture that makes them want to stay.

The moral of the story is, be good to your reps and they'll be good to you. Never view them as "threats to your job," nor as disposable if things don't go your way.

Every rep has a unique voice, that's why you hired individuals and not drones. Give them the autonomy to contribute to the company by encouraging them to contribute to the team. Provide parameters, not barriers.

***

Hiring Sales Reps

Finding the Unicorn of Cannabis Sales Reps

Here's an example for you, I love donuts, but just because I love donuts doesn't make me the best candidate to sell them. You might be wondering why my passion for donuts would make me say that I'm not qualified. The reality is, my passion for a product has nothing to do with my passion for the people and company who make them. Do I honestly want to know what goes into making and running a donut company? Not really. My passion is in consuming donuts. Same goes for cannabis. Passion for consuming cannabis doesn't mean that the individual has the desire to learn all there is to know about how your company produces products and takes them to market. To the layman, sales is "easy" and "fun." As I mentioned before, sales is about educating people who want to know about your company and brand. A passion for the product is simply the first step. Wanting to dive much, much deeper takes a unique personality, one that wants to dive into the culture and network of cannabis. All of this takes time, knowledge, dedication, and a lot of patience and savvy. So, how do you find this magical rep that has the desire to fit into a culture that just emerged from an underground movement?

You pay them, that's how.

Sales reps must have a base salary, especially if you're looking for a solid rep who will perform. The attitude that reps can make a lot of money in commission is all just your perception of the reception of your product. Note I said, "your perception," which means it has nothing to do with actual facts. Sales is the front line of your business, and you should treat it with as much respect as you do your own position. Reps are not "a dime a dozen," they are an asset, and necessary part of your business, treat them as such.

As you're structuring your budgets, consider how important sales reps and sales materials (such as stickers, lanyards, etc.) are to the mission. Don't drop all of your money on creating the product, make sure your company is scalable. If you're just starting out, start small and increase production with the demand. Take advantage of economies of scale discounts, by purchasing more swag items at lower costs. Trust me, this investment will not goto waste. Sales is the face of your brand and requires company resources. Make sure you're paying your reps a modest salary, something almost livable, and let that incentivize them to earn their commissions. As I stated earlier, be sure that your cost of goods includes a percentage of commission payable to your rep for gaining the business. If you want quality from your reps, you must have the resources to hire the caliber of rep you need. You must also have the time to allow them to make their mark. One thing many people don't realize is that even though sales reps often make good money in other industries, rarely do cannabis outside sales jobs pay well, and being a sales rep is expensive. The travel time, wear and tear on their cars, in an effort for no salary and low commissions is not desirable, nor is it motivating. Even if you reimburse for mileage, it's rarely enough to cover all the costs. Be mindful of this. High turn over in sales reps reflects poorly on a company, and this is sure to happen if you're offering "commission only."

Unlike the unicorn, sales isn't magical, it takes time to gain traction, and requires resources, so make sure you have them.

***

I know I keep repeating this next statement, but it's simply because I still hear the common misnomer that sales is "fun" and reps rarely work. What management must realize is that sales is fun, but it *is* work. Sure, going to industry events that are basically one big party is fun, but is it really "fun" when you're required to set up a booth an hour early after working all day, talk to customers promoting products from 6pm - 11pm, only to spend another hour tearing down, driving home, getting to bed at 1am, and then getting up and doing it all over again at 8am? Trust me, reps would much rather attend the events as a consumer and have fun with their friends, and often times they make better connections this way than "manning a booth." So just because they're at an industry event "having fun" they are most definitely, still "at work."

***
Being a Cannabis Sales Rep

Here's the part where I speak to sales reps, both current and prospective

In any industry, sales reps must speak 1,000 languages. If you're a seasoned sales rep with a proven track record, I'd consider putting this attribute on your resume. The reality is, you must be relatable to everyone, and know how to modify your approach to even the most difficult of clients. In sales, literally, everyone must like you, your career depends on it. But you want to work in cannabis sales. Cannabis is a culture of various generations; people from all walks of life. In your travels, you will obviously meet your clients, but you will also likely meet their customers. You will meet so many different people who embody everyone from 20-somethings to senior citizens looking for pain relief. You must be able to speak to each of them in the language they understand. You almost have to be psychic, you can add that to your resume too, as you have to be able to read them. Assess each individual, well, individually. Read their face, note how they dress, how they hold themselves, how do they look at you? Based on all of this, what is the best approach, what will be the next words out of your mouth? It all happens in a split second, and yes, you must be *that* good. This is what makes sales so much fun but it is also what makes sales mentally exhausting. If you can successfully do this, you will set yourself above your competition. It will undoubtedly make an impression on your clients and cast a positive light on you. These are basic traits of a sales rep. Sales is a personality, not just anyone can do it.

Cannabis users and industry professionals are passionate about this plant. You will never know everything, in any industry, so learn as much as you can and make sure that sales is the right fit for you. You may find that you'll be more successful working in a grow and learning more about the process of cannabis, before you launch into outside sales. There's a lot you can learn by doing outside sales, but if you've never sold before, you'll quickly find that there's a lot to learn about sales strategies, sales cycles, company missions, company dynamics, the list goes on an on. The bottom line is, expect a sales position to consume your life, even when you're on vacation. If you're not sure that your current skillset will assist you in meeting the sales goals of the company, start somewhere else and *learn*.

Let's say, that after all of this, you're still interested in doing outside sales in the cannabis industry. You land an interview with a company you truly want to learn more about and potentially represent, and you knock it out of the park! Congratulations! Before you graciously accept their offer of employment, or a contract position, please, do the following - Google everyone with whom you interview. You don't want to find yourself in a position working for unscrupulous people. You'll often find that some people in cannabis have paid the price of working or using cannabis when it was illegal, I personally don't think this is an issue. But if you find that your company is being run or funded by convicted white collar criminals, you'd be best to know this before you accept a position. Integrity is everything. Knowing who you work for will undoubtedly reflect in your performance.

Used Car Salesmen Need Not Apply

I really wish I didn't have to say this, but please, if you sold used cars, leave those strategies at the door. Used car salesmen have had a bad reputation for decades and this is the worst kind of salesman for outside cannabis sales. No one likes to be hustled and the "wheel and deal" technique is simply gross. Talk to people as people, not as a quick buck. There's a sales cycle that goes into cannabis. You could luck out and make a sale on your first attempt, if they've already tried your company's product, but it's more realistic to expect a sales cycle of at least 4 - 6 weeks. If you're pitching a product, they will want to sample it. Your first, or even your second, visit will likely not result in a sale. But if you follow my upcoming advice, they may just agree to try your products, and that's a big accomplishment. So make sure that everything you've said about your brand can and will be delivered when they try them. Then it's all about follow up and building a relationship that makes people want to work with *you*, which is the benefit to your company.

Once you get positive feedback on your product and secure an order, you can begin to let them know that larger deals for less money per unit are available, but watch your technique. Let it be the dispensary's decision whether or not to buy, not because you've backed them into a corner and they can't get out. Offer your support, an "I'll do everything I can to help you sell our product" attitude is more respected and appreciated. Remember, they're the ones taking the risk on you. Once you close the deal, the hard work begins. If your product doesn't sell, the likelihood of repeat business is out the window. Take your time, have integrity, build trust, engage with customers, this is the foundation the industry functions upon.

Remember when I talked about Pop-Ups? These types of events put you in front of both dispensary staff and their customers. Dispensaries are a place of calm, "chill" vibes. If you're hustling their customers, making them feel uncomfortable and pressed for a sale, there's a good likelihood that you, or even worse, your company, won't be welcomed back for a Pop Up anytime soon. Be gentle with people, make them want to come back and try your products, when they can do it comfortably and on their schedule. Again, this isn't about the quick sale, it's about relationships. If a dispensary's customers love you, they will talk about you with the staff with fondness. That's what you're cultivating, positive images of you and the company you represent.

Actually Being a Cannabis Sales Rep

If you're still with me at this point, you might just be cut out to be an outside sales rep in the cannabis industry. So now I need to give you an overview of *how* to actually be a cannabis sales rep, and then I'll talk about some of the more finite details of the job.

Keep in mind that initial interactions are your "first impressions." The "gatekeepers," who, as the name implies, are the first people you see when you walk into a dispensary. They are the ones you need to become your best friends, but let it be genuine and not contrived. Remember, you're not a phony, you're a sales rep who gets to know everyone and enjoys doing it. The gatekeepers know you're looking for business, and honestly, that's irrelevant on your first call. Get to know people, that's what sales reps do, that's how we build our reputations, and that's how we get to the people we need to talk to.

- Always be friendly, and upbeat. Just because you've been working all day doesn't mean you carry your exhaustion with you. "Hi! How's it goin?" with a smile always goes far. Dispensaries see hundreds of customers and many reps everyday, their employees are at work, just like you, so be considerate of this.
- Never be a nuisance. If you see that a dispensary is busy, politely slip your card on the counter and say, "I just wanted to pop by and introduce myself. I'll swing by again."
- If you're lucky enough to have a moment with the "gatekeeper," ask how they are and *briefly* make small talk. You don't want to get them in trouble for not doing their other duties, and you don't want to look bad for holding up a line. Always step aside if a customer comes in and let them do their job. Customers always go in front of you, even if you're in the middle of closing a deal.
- Once you've made your impression on the gatekeeper, let them know that you're a new rep for "such and such" company and was wondering if a manager had a moment to chat. If they say, "No," never get discouraged. A reply like, "No worries! I totally get it," goes far. Simply follow up with, "Is there a better time for me to swing by?" This is also a great opportunity to get their manager's (or whoever does the purchasing) contact information and send an email follow up (I'll go into how to best perform email follow ups in just a moment).
- A good rule of thumb for follow up calls is 1.5 - 2 weeks, unless you hear otherwise, or schedule a meeting. But about 2 weeks in non-invasive and considerate to your prospective clients.

- When you're lucky enough to get to the right person, make small talk. Make your business dealings seem secondary. Remember, cannabis is personal and you're looking for a relationship first and business second. If this is your first visit, you're hoping to get them to agree to receiving samples. So simply take stock of the products they carry and complement them, if the opportunity presents. Then you can say, "My company has some great new products, would it be OK if I sent you some samples?" If they agree, get the necessary information your company needs to send the samples, i.e.: license numbers, address, name of person to receive, etc. If they decline, that's OK. This gives you the opportunity to stop back by in a couple of weeks and continue building a relationship.
- Be aware at all times the tone of the conversation - is it rushed, is it casual? Be courteous to the cues the staff is giving you. You never want to be viewed as the rep that "just won't leave."
- Keep it short and sweet. Once you have approval to send samples, let them get back to work. If you don't see an opening to gain approval, use it as a reason to follow up in the next week or so.

If you're given a manager's email to follow up this is a great way to never get a response. You can take the opportunity to send an email to simply introduce yourself, and remember to get the name of the person with whom you spoke (I'll list the basics of what information to gather in the next few pages). A follow-up email is a way for you and your brand to gain a little awareness, but not the appropriate time to ask for business. An example email would be:

Hi Sam,

My name is "X" and I'm with "such and such" company. I stopped by your store today and had a great conversation with "so and so." You weren't available when I stopped by, so I just wanted to take this opportunity to introduce myself and see if there was a good time to come by and chat. Just let me know. Thanks so much!

It's literally that simple and non-invasive.

Let's fast-forward to a time when you've finally gotten approval to send samples to a client. Here's how to follow up and take the conversation to the next level of sales.

- Know when the samples were received by the dispensary, and give them a week to get them divided out among the staff and

allow time for feedback. Most dispensaries have a team process for judging samples.
- When you do follow up, speak with the individual who approved you sending the samples and ask if they had a chance to give them a try.
- If they say yes, ask what they thought of them. Never be insulted by mediocre feedback. Everyone is different and everyone has different preferences, and you can say just that. Our differences are what make life fun and keeps things interesting. If a dispensary doesn't like your product, the reality is, they won't be the best candidates to sell it to their customers. But this isn't the end of the road. Maintain your follow-ups, but perhaps not as frequently. You're building your reputation, as well as your company's. You never know when a "No" will turn into a "Yes."
- If everyone simply loves your product, then you're in luck. But that doesn't necessarily mean they're ready to order today. Budgets dictate, shelf-space dictates, your product's shelf-life dictates…so many variables come into play. Stay aware and maintain your reputation. It will turn into a sale with diligence.
- If you've hit the jackpot and they place their first order, it's your time to shine! Schedule a Pop Up, and make sure you show up. (See the section on Pop Ups and Used Car Salesmen.) You want to support their investment with your company, because the reality is, they're banking on you to help get their customers introduced and excited about this new addition. This is not the time to "hit them up" for a big sale with bulk discounts. You'll know when the appropriate time for that arises.

Also keep in mind that your relationships in the cannabis industry will go beyond your point of contact at dispensaries or other clients. Sales reps must learn about cannabis customers. Often times, dispensaries are located right next door to one another, or even across the street. You'll quickly find that even in such close proximity, each dispensary's customers come from various demographics, and it is your obligation to listen and learn their unique needs. This will help you modify your pitch to properly meet the needs of your customers, individually.

A Sales Rep's Book of Business

I touched on this topic previously, in the Sales Management CRM section of this handbook. As you begin to develop yourself and your reputation in cannabis, you are inadvertently building your personal "book of business." It is expected that you report your contacts to your employer, but what your employer doesn't own is your relationships. People become part of *your* network, you become recognizable at industry events, or even at the grocery store. This is where sales becomes personal and makes you valuable to your employer, and prospective employers. Your network becomes part of your competitive edge. It's not something to brag about, it's something you should protect. It's your name that is becoming valuable, so think about how you want people to know you.

If the opportunity presents on your first visit, make sure you get the dispensary's business card. Often times dispensary employees will write the name and email of your appropriate contact on the back. Whether you have their business card or not, the basic information you will need for your knowledge and any CRM is:

- Dispensary Name
- Dispensary Address, Phone, and General Email
- Contact's Name
- Contact's Email
- Who You Spoke with on each visit
- Pertinent Details of your interactions and conversations
- Feedback/Concerns/Questions on Products

Here's my advice on how to manage your interactions on sales calls, which will lead to you making a solid name for yourself in the cannabis industry:

- Actively listen to your customers, repeat back to them so they know you understand what they need
- Never be too proud to say, "I don't know, but I'll find out" - better to take a little more time than make a mistake that is costly to your customer, and threaten your business
- Always follow up with customers, no matter how big or small the orders
- Don't make promises you can't keep, or don't want to keep
- Never embellish your product's attributes
- Never make health claims about cannabis products
- Go the extra mile for your customers
- Make sure the customer knows you are his/her advocate for your company
- If there's a problem, take the lead and fix it
- Be diplomatic when solving problems, you represent your customer and your company
- Choose your words carefully
- Respectfully challenge your company if you see that your customer was shorted/wronged
- If you modify the sales pitch and find something that works, share it with your team
- Never bad mouth your competition

- Numbers are everything, be prepared to answer for your performance

Numbers, Numbers, Numbers

Here's another repetition on my part. Sales reps are judged by numbers, but it is the rep's job to have a solid understanding of their business, territory dynamics, and company expectations. It's the rep's job to protect themselves with facts, not opinions. As much as I've tried to enforce, in the first section of this handbook, that companies shouldn't be hasty nor emotional when developing sales goals, and not allow poorly structured numbers explain the effectiveness of the rep, a solid and savvy sales rep will always bring facts to the table to support their numbers, good or bad. So keep track of your own accounts, sales numbers, develop your own spreadsheets which indicate your productivity. DO NOT rely on the company's CRM to track this for you, as I previously stated, this is about you developing your own reputation and protecting yourself.

I've often seen companies attempt to blame the reps because they couldn't single handedly save the company because the business plan reflects unrealistic expectations. So, in an effort to be proactive, do your own research, be open and engaged with your management. As with anything, it's always better to be proactive than reactive.

***

In Closing

There are millions of people who want into this unique industry, seeing dollar signs. The perception in the general public is that cannabis is a "cash cow," you will quickly find that it isn't. The price of flower fluctuates, customer traffic fluctuates, there are so many variables to consider (i.e.: is your territory medical sales only, or are recreational sales legal, does your territory rely heavily on tourism traffic, etc.) Remember, there is no cross-state transportation in cannabis just yet, but when there is, we will see things become more like grocery store distribution. Until then, please remember that you must navigate within your state's regulations, demand for your product (i.e.: edible, concentrate, etc.), dispensary shelf-space, etc.

Companies perceive that dispensaries are raking in the dough, but keep in mind that their expenses are paid without any tax deductions - everything comes out of the cash they bring in. The taxes are high, the licensing is expensive, the compliance checks are expensive, they spend a lot of what they bring in. So based on all of this, be respectful and be prepared for hearing the word "No"…a lot. The good news is, cannabis is an ever changing landscape. So you have the advantage of just stopping by to say, "Hi," not asking for business every single time, and building a relationship that will likely yield a sale in the near future.

I know I've said a lot in this handbook, and I could probably say a lot more, but there is one key sales technique that will help you in any industry and on any sales call.

Be kind to your competition

Sales reps can get a very bad name if they go around bad mouthing the competition. Cannabis is a very "friendly competition" environment. The resounding theme is,

We're all in this together

Everyone has tried a lot of different products, and they all have their unique place. Complement other brands, try saying things like, "We all do something similar, we just like to think we do it better." You'll be surprised how far being positive will get you when it comes to building a good name for yourself, in any industry.

***

My hope is that each of you finds the success and fulfillment you seek from your career in cannabis. I truly hope that this little handbook will help guide companies to better interactions with their sales teams, and raise the bar on the expectations sales reps have from their companies, as well. Best of luck to you all!

RESOURCES:

I thought you might like a couple of names of cannabis industry professionals that know many of the rules and themes of the cannabis industry. They might be a bit more expensive than on-line suppliers, but I promise you, their output is extremely worth it.

Remember - cannabis has an image, and it's all about the swag, make sure your brand stands out and matches the culture you're trying to reach.

Top Shelf Printing - www.topshelfprinters.com - Pins, Hats, Water Bottles, and practically anything else you can imagine.

Label Tec, Inc - www.labeltecinc.com - Stickers, labels, and cannabis industry packaging.

www.ingramcontent.com/pod-product-compliance
Lightning Source LLC
Chambersburg PA
CBHW031505210526
45463CB00003B/1089